Yeats in Love

Yeats in Love

by Annie West

NEW ISLAND

YEATS IN LOVE

First published 2014 by New Island

16 Priory Office Park, Stillorgan, County Dublin

www.newisland.ie

Copyright © Annie West, 2014

Annie West has asserted her moral rights.

PRINT ISBN: 978-1-84840-392-5

EPUB ISBN: 978-1-84840-393-2

MOBI ISBN: 978-1-84840-394-9

British Library Cataloguing Data. A CIP catalogue record for this
book is available from the British Library

Typeset by Amy West *amywest.ie*

Cover design by Amy West *amywest.ie*

Printed by

New Island received financial assistance from the Arts Council.
(an Comhairle Ealaíon) 70 Merrion Square, Dublin 2, Ireland

1 *"My world was fallen and over, for your dark soft eyes on it shone;*
A thousand years it had waited and now it is gone, it is gone."

William Butler Yeats, c. 1891

2　"Yeats never had the remotest idea of taking care of himself. He would go all day without food unless someone remembered it for him, and in the same way would go on eating unless someone checked him. That first winter, a hard one, he would come to see me—five miles from Dublin, striding along over the snow-bound roads, a gaunt young figure, mouthing poetry, swinging his arms and gesticulating as he went. George Russell complained to me the other day that Willie Yeats had said somewhere of him, and printed it, that he used to walk about the streets of Dublin swinging his arms like a flail, unconscious of the alarm and bewilderment of passers-by. It was Willie's own case. I remember how the big Dublin policemen used to eye him in those days, as though uncertain whether to 'run him in' or not. But, by and by, they used to say, 'Shure, 'tisn't mad he is, nor yet drink taken. 'Tis the poethry that's disturbin' his head,' and leave him alone."

Katharine Tynan, 1913

Contents

Foreword

Becoming an adult means, or should mean, among other things, learning to distinguish between loving another and being 'in love' as understood by adolescents. I am perfectly prepared to believe that Yeats was 'in love' with Maud Gonne when a young man, but have come more and more to the view that he never loved her as an adult might love another. This is absurd, in a way, since none but the two involved in a relationship can ever really hope to understand with any confidence the dynamic between two people. Nevertheless, the enduring fascination with Gonne that Yeats kept alive into his late poems seems to me a willed thing rather than an authentic passion of the loving heart. A genuine passion it very likely was, when both were young, and it is clear that some bond between them endured as long as they both lived—but Maud gave her heart elsewhere, and there is no evidence in the poems that Yeats had ever an adult understanding of this, any more than he is likely to have reflected on her right to command and direct her own affections and passions. There is, of course, something finally endearing about an old man maintaining some loyalty to the scalded, elated heart of his youth—but something sad, too, since that resolute backward gaze tells us Yeats was unable, or perhaps unwilling, to accept that Maud had grown into her own life and separate destiny. I would be more persuaded that he loved her if there were poems that speak in love and affection to her own full, independent life as she chose to live it. None of this matters when it comes to the poems we have, since a poem is neither biography nor autobiography and must be valued for itself, but I do sometimes yearn for the poems Yeats might have written for and to the actual adult woman he could have loved as a grown man.

On the other hand, nothing attracts the imp of comedy as readily as does high seriousness—as long as it's the high seriousness of someone else. Leafing through Annie West's images here, two things struck me. The first is that it is indeed possible to find a gentle comedy in Yeats's professed lifelong infatuation; the second is that perhaps, after all, the old boy was putting it on a bit. Young love has been the stuff of comedy since hormonal imbalance first announced itself, and I doubt there will be a single person leafing through this book who has not some rueful memory of how ridiculous they must have seemed to others when first they fell in love. Annie captures that first high foolishness very well, I think, but she captures equally well the comedy of what happens when a mature poet like Yeats, wilful, self-centred and with a grand notion of himself, decides to put his youthful passion on life support, intending to harvest as many poems as possible from the unwilling, sometimes unconscious, donor.

It is possible to say that there is something very silly about Willy 'in love', about the prolongation into late life of a tempest that had very likely blown itself out by the time he'd reached thirty. The paradox, of course, is that he may not have loved Maud with the high seriousness proposed by the poems, but he managed to make real love poems, enduring and convincing poems, out of the whole dubious business. Which may have been all he cared about, or all that should, finally, concern us.

What does it matter, in the end, whether you know or I know if Yeats 'really' loved Maud? What's it to us? Annie's gentle humour sends us out past the high seriousness of presuming to judge the truth of the matter, back to the poems themselves, with a sense that Yeats was, as Auden put it, "silly like us", but a supreme love poet for all that.

Theo Dorgan, 2014

Introduction

Asked by a fourth-class pupil:

"Why do you always make fun of William Butler Yeats?"

Well. Somebody has to do it.

I ought to be a Yeats scholar and know his poetry inside out, living as I do in the heart of Yeats country. My grandmother played the church organ at his funeral. Everywhere in Sligo there are monuments to Yeats, from statues to restaurants to football clubs. I had always found the deification of Yeats somewhat hard to follow, since my relationship with the Nobel Laureate was irretrievably soured in a Dublin secondary school by a teacher who clearly not only disliked me, and all my friends, but also Yeats, all literature, English in general, and the whole entire process of teaching.

By the time I emerged from school, blinking and gasping, with my (not hugely impressive) Leaving Cert in my hand, I vowed never to open another poetry book again. Things took a turn for the better in the nineties, when I moved to Sligo and was given the job of Church Warden at St Columba's Church, Drumcliffe. As a result I got to meet many visiting Yeats scholars who unwittingly assisted in my imminent rehabilitation by recounting stories of Willie Yeats and his Muse. The Muse who made him great. It was on a gloomy day in March when I happened to meet Stella Mew, the then president of the Yeats Society. What started as a short conversation became a very long one. Stella is the most erudite Yeats scholar, but has a charming and delightful side of mischief. After a long chat I ran back to my drawing board and began what I thought was one single cartoon strip. I began to read about Yeats and Maud Gonne. His hopeless pursuit. His four marriage proposals. How he waited for Iseult to grow up and then proposed to her as well. And how she turned him down too.

Somehow, I had missed this remarkable, painful, yet amusing story. It started slowly: just one illustration, a comic strip where Yeats meets Maud Gonne for the first time. I thought that was it, but then more started coming. Ideas arrived in my head by themselves, with no prompting at all.

I realised quite early on I could almost always reduce each scenario into one single image. Before long I had four images. Then six. The *Yeats in Love* series grew and grew, and culminated in a touring exhibition which was opened in Dublin for the first time in 2008 by Senator David Norris. As the years went by people began to send me funny stories and quotes by or about Willy. I read books about the love story, even the one-sided love letters, ignoring all else as a distraction. The one thing I wanted to be sure of was that this story would, although embellished to a ridiculous degree, have a solid basis in fact. I wandered down many side roads while making this series, but many images were discarded because they weren't real or likely to be. Then, my interpretation of his poetry was simply based on the way I used to annoy my English teacher: I took every word literally. Many detentions were imposed over an argument about where exactly his ladder went, et cetera. Since that murky day in Drumcliffe with Stella in 2007, I find I have, without noticing, rehabilitated myself after the trauma of that mind-numbing secondary education. I am, nearly, at peace with my Yeats. During my research I read much about Maud Gonne and how mean she was to him. Curiously, in ten years I have found myself feeling a bit sorry for Willy. I never thought I would hear myself saying that. But here we are, ten years later and friends at last.

Annie West, 2014

3   "… a tall, lanky boy with deep-set dark eyes behind glasses, over which a lock of dark hair was constantly falling, to be pushed back impatiently by long sensitive fingers, often stained with paint – dressed in shabby clothes…"

Maud Gonne, 1889

Another Valentine's Day Party ruined

4 *The Young Man's Song*

I whispered, "I am too young,"
And then, "I am old enough";
Wherefore I threw a penny
To find out if I might love.
"Go and love, go and love, young man,
If the lady be young and fair,"
Ah, penny, brown penny, brown penny,
I am looped in the loops of her hair.

Oh, love is the crooked thing,
There is nobody wise enough
To find out all that is in it,
For he would be thinking of love
Till the stars had run away,
And the shadows eaten the moon.
Ah, penny, brown penny, brown penny,
One cannot begin it too soon.

William Butler Yeats, 1916

W. B. Yeats meets Maud Gonne for the first time

5 "Miss Gonne, the Dublin beauty (who is marching on to glory over the hearts of the Dublin youths) called today on Willie, of course, but also apparently on Papa. She is immensely tall and very stylish and well dressed in a careless way. She came in a hansom all the way from Belgravia and kept the hansom waiting while she was here. Lily noticed that she was in her slippers. She has a rich complexion and hazel eyes and is, I think, decidedly handsome.
I could not see her well as her face was turned from me…"

Lolly Yeats, 1889

Maud Gonne goes for a little swim

6 "I was twenty-three years old when the troubling of my life began. I had heard
from time to time in letters from Miss O'Leary, John O'Leary's old sister, of
a beautiful girl who had left the society of the Viceregal Court for Dublin
nationalism. In after years I persuaded myself that I felt premonitory excitement
at the first reading of her name. Presently she drove up to our house in Bedford
Park ... I had never thought to see in
a living woman so great beauty. It belonged to famous pictures, to poetry,
to some legendary past. A complexion like the blossom of apples, and yet face and
body had the beauty of lineaments which Blake calls the highest beauty because it
changes least from youth to age, and a stature so great that she seemed of a divine
race. Her movements were worthy of her
form, and I understood at last why the poet of antiquity, where we
would but speak of face and form, sings, loving some lady, that she
paces like a goddess."

William Butler Yeats, 1913

Pallas Athene

7   "In the next few years I saw her always when she passed to and fro between Dublin and Paris, surrounded, no matter how rapid her journey and how brief her stay at either end of it, by cages full of birds, canaries, finches
of all kinds, dogs, a parrot, and once a full-grown hawk from Donegal.
Once when I saw her to her railway carriage I noticed how the cages obstructed racks and cushions and wondered what her fellow-travellers would say, but the carriage remained empty. It was years before I could see into the mind that lay hidden under so much beauty and so much energy."

William Butler Yeats, 1922

Yeats proposes to Maud Gonne for the first time

8 *A Poet to His Beloved*

I bring you with reverent hands
The books of my numberless dreams;
White woman that passion has worn
As the tide nears the dove-grey sands,
And with heart more old than the horn
That is brimmed from the pale fire of time;
White woman with numberless dreams
I bring you my passionate rhyme.

William Butler Yeats, 1899

Overthrown by a woman's gaze

9 "[Yeats was] all dreams and gentleness… beautiful to look at with his dark face, its touch of vivid colouring, the night black hair, the eager dark eyes. He wore a queer little beard in those days… he lived, breathed, drank and slept poetry."

Katharine Tynan, 1913

Maud Gonne goes shopping

10 "Did I tell you how much I admire Maud Gonne?… If she said the world was flat or the moon an old caubeen tossed up into the sky I would be proud to be of her party."

William Butler Yeats to **Ellen O'Leary**, 1889

"Of course , my dear. You have my undivided attention"

11 *The White Birds*

I would that we were, my beloved, white birds on the foam of the sea!
We tire of the flame of the meteor, before it can fade and flee;
And the flame of the blue star of twilight, hung low on the rim of the sky,
Has awakened in our hearts, my beloved, a sadness that may not die.
A weariness comes from those dreamers,
dew-dabbled, the lily and rose;
Ah, dream not of them, my beloved, the flame of the meteor that goes,
Or the flame of the blue star that lingers hung low in the fall of the dew:
For I would we were changed to white birds on the wandering foam:
I and you!
I am haunted by numberless islands, and many a Danaan shore,
Where Time would surely forget us, and Sorrow come near us no more;
Soon far from the rose and the lily, and fret of the flames would we be,
Were we only white birds, my beloved, buoyed out on the foam of the sea!

William Butler Yeats, 1892

Never give all the heart

12 "She is not only handsome but very clever…she is very Irish, a kind of 'Diana of the Crossways'. Her pet monkey was making, much of the time, little melancholy cries at the hearthrug…There were also two young pigeons in a cage, whom I mistook for sparrows."

William Butler Yeats to **John O'Leary**, 1889

She loves me not. She loves me. She loves me not.

13 "… then I realised who she was… She was a legend to us young persons in our teens … Her height would have drawn attention anywhere, but it was her beauty that produced the most startling effect. It was startling in its greatness, its dignity, its strangeness. Supreme beauty is so rare that its first effect is a kind of shock."

"… People's hearts stopped beating [at her] marvellous beauty, her height and the memories of her militant patriotism."

Mary Colum, 1902

Yeats on a train

14 "He has above all, a weird appearance, which is triumphant with middle aged masculine women, and a dictatorial manner which is irresistible with the considerable bevy of female and male mediocrities interested in intellectual things."

Edward Martyn, 1914

W. B. Yeats pitches an idea to David O. Selznick

15 "I saw much of Maud Gonne and my hope renewed again. If I could go
   to her and prove, by putting my hand in the fire till I had burnt it badly,
   would not that make her understand that devotion like mine should
   [not] be thrown away lightly. Often as I went to see her I had this thought
   in my mind and I do not think that it was fear of pain that prevented me but fear
   of being mad. I wonder at moments if I was not really mad."

William Butler Yeats,1914

Maud Gonne delivers another impassioned speech

16 "… not only because she was beautiful, but because that beauty suggested joy and freedom. Besides, there was an element in her beauty that moved minds full of old Gaelic stories and poems, for she looked as though she lived in an ancient civilization where all superiorities whether of the mind or the body were part of a public ceremonial, were in some way the crowd's creation, as the entrance of the Pope into Saint Peter's is the crowd's creation. Her beauty backed by her great stature could instantly affect an assembly… for it was incredibly distinguished, and… her face, like the face
of some Greek statue, showed little thought, her whole body seemed a master-work of long labouring thought, as though a Scopas had measured and calculated, consorted with Egyptian sages, and mathematicians out of Babylon, that he might outface even Artemisia's sepulchral image with a living norm."

William Butler Yeats, 1914

Joyce tells Yeats what he's doing wrong

17 "… tortured by physical desire and disappointed love. Often as I walked in the woods at Coole, it would have been a relief to have screamed aloud."

William Butler Yeats, 1914

Yeats realises the wisdom in being careful what you wish for

18 *He Wishes for the Cloths of Heaven*

Had I the heavens' embroidered cloths,
Enwrought with golden and silver light,
The blue and the dim and the dark cloths
Of night and light and the half-light,
I would spread the cloths under your feet:
But I, being poor, have only my dreams;
I have spread my dreams under your feet;
Tread softly because you tread on my dreams.

William Butler Yeats, 1889

Yeats receives an answer to his second marriage proposal

19　*The Arrow*

I thought of your beauty, and this arrow,
Made out of a wild thought, is in my marrow.
There's no man may look upon her, no man,
As when newly grown to be a woman,
Tall and noble but with face and bosom
Delicate in colour as apple blossom.
This beauty's kinder, yet for a reason
I could weep that the old is out of season.

William Butler Yeats, 1903

Yeats meets Oscar Wilde and defines the term "Cruel irony"

20 "Sometimes, when I had gone to sleep with the endeavour to send my soul to that of Maud Gonne, using some symbol, which I forget, I would wake dreaming of a shower of precious stones. Sometimes she would have some corresponding experience in Paris and upon the same night. […] I thought we became one in a world of emotion eternalised by its own intensity and purity, and that this world had for its symbol precious stones. No physical, sexual sensation ever accompanied those dreams."

William Butler Yeats, 1889

Yeats arrives at Maud Gonne's house to propose for the third time

21 "Oh, Maud, why don't you marry me and give up this tragic struggle and
    live a peaceful life? I could make such a beautiful life for you among
    Artists and Writers who would understand you."

    "Willie, are you not tired of asking that question? How often have I told
    you to thank the Gods that I will not marry you. You would not be happy with
    me."

    "I am not happy without you."

    "Oh, yes you are, because you make beautiful poetry out of what you call your
    unhappiness and you are happy in that. Marriage would be such a dull affair.
    Poets should never marry. The world should thank me for
    not marrying you."

Maud Gonne and **William Butler Yeats**, 1914

W. B. Yeats sends a greeting to John MacBride

WHY should I blame her that she filled my days
With misery, or that she would of late
Have taught to ignorant men most violent ways,
Or hurled the little streets upon the great,
Had they but courage equal to desire?
What could have made her peaceful with a mind
That nobleness made simple as a fire,
With beauty like a tightened bow, a kind
That is not natural in an age like this,
Being high and solitary and most stern?
Why, what could she have done, being what she is?
Was there another Troy for her to burn?

William Butler Yeats, 1916

Maud. Gonne.

Never give all the heart, for love
Will hardly seem worth thinking of
To passionate women if it seem
Certain, and they never dream
That it fades out from kiss to kiss;
For everything that's lovely is
But a brief, dreamy, kind delight.
O never give the heart outright,
For they, for all smooth lips can say,
Have given their hearts up to the play.
And who could play it well enough
If deaf and dumb and blind with love?
He that made this knows all the cost,
For he gave all his heart and lost.

William Butler Yeats, 1904

W. B. Yeats attends Maud Gonne's Wedding

24 *He Wishes His Beloved Were Dead*

Were you but lying cold and dead,
And lights were paling out of the West,
You would come hither, and bend your head,
And I would lay my head on your breast;
And you would murmur tender words,
Forgiving me, because you were dead:
Nor would you rise and hasten away,
Though you have the will of wild birds,
But know your hair was bound and wound
About the stars and moon and sun:
O would, beloved, that you lay
Under the dock-leaves in the ground,
While lights were paling one by one.

William Butler Yeats, 1899

W. B. Yeats proposes to Maud Gonne for the fourth time

25 "At first every man on whom she looked was in love with her…I remember when the heads of all my male friends, young and old, were flustered by her beauty and her grace. But they soon got over it. I have always held that love must have something to live upon, something of invitation if not of response. Her aloofness must have chilled the most ardent lover."

Katharine Tynan, 1889

If Maud Gonne had said yes

26 "What end will it all have? I fear for her and for myself. She has all myself.
I was never more deeply in love, but my desires must go elsewhere if I would
escape their poison. I am in constant terror of some entanglement parting us, and
all the while I know that she made me and I her. She is my innocence and I her
wisdom. Of old she was a Phoenix and I feared her, but now she is my child more
than my sweetheart."

William Butler Yeats, 1889

Time can but make it easier to be wise

27 "As for Willie Yeats I love him dearly as a friend but
I could not for one minute imagine marrying him."

Maud Gonne to her sister, 1902

Notes

1   My world was fallen and over... Yeats, W. B., from *'Cycles Ago: In Memory of Your Dream One Night'* (unpublished). Cited in MacBride White, Anna (Author) and Jeffares, A. Norman (editor) {1994}, *The Gonne–Yeats Letters 1893–1938* (Syracuse University Press), p. 20.

2   Yeats never had the remotest idea... Katharine Tynan, cited in Sarker, Sunil Kumar {1997}, *W.B. Yeats: Poetry and Plays* (Atlantic Publishers & Distributors Pvt Ltd), p. 19.

3   A tall, lanky boy... MacBride, Maud Gonne {1913}, *A Servant of the Queen: Reminiscences* (University of Chicago Press) p. 319.

4   'The Young Man's Song', Yeats, W. B. {1910}, *The Green Helmet, and Other Poems* (The Macmillan Company) p. 37.

5   Miss Gonne, the Dublin Beauty... Lolly Yeats's diary entry for 30 January 1889, cited in Smith, Stan {1990}, *W.B. Yeats: A Critical Introduction* (Rowland & Littlefield) p. 35.

6   I was twenty-three years old... Yeats, W. B. {written 1916–1917, published 1972}, cited in Finneran, Richard J. (ed.) {2002} *The Yeats Reader: A Portable Compendium of Poetry, Drams and Prose* (Palgrave MacMillan) p. 106.

7   In the next few years I saw her... Yeats, W. B. {1916-36}, *Autobiographies, Book I: four years 1887–1891* (originally from *The Trembling of the Veil*, 1922)

8   'A Poet to His Beloved', Yeats, W. B. {1899}, *The Wind Among the Reeds* (Elkin Matthews), p. 29.

9   All dreams and gentleness... Tynan, Katharine {1913}, *Twenty-Five Years: Reminiscences* (Smith, Elder & Co) p. 145.

10   Did I tell you how... Levenson, S. {1889}, *A Biography of Yeats' Beloved Maud Gonne*, (M. W. Books) p. 57.

11   'The White Birds' Yeats, W. B. {1994 }*The collected poems of W. B. Yeats* (Wordsworth Editions) p. 33.

12   She is not only handsome... Cited in Ellmann, Richard {1948} *Yeats: The Man and the Masks* (W. W. Norton & company), p. 104.

13   Then I realised who she was... Colum, Mary {1947} *Life and the Dream* (Macmillan), p. 182.

14   He has above all, a weird appearance... Martyn, Edward {1914} 'A Plea for the Revival of the Irish Literary Theatre' (*The Irish Review (Dublin)* Vol. 4, No. 38), pp. 79–84.

15   I saw much of Maud Gonne... Yeats, W. B. {1956} *Memoirs* (Macmillan), p. 105.

16   Not only because she... Yeats, W. B. {1956} *Autobiographies, Book V, The Stirring of the Bones* (Macmillan), p. 365.

17   Tortured by physical desire... Yeats, W. B. {1972} *Memoirs* (Macmillan), p. 125.

18   'He Wishes for the Cloths of Heaven', Yeats, W. B., {1899} *The Wind Among the Reeds* (Elkin Matthews), p. 60.

19   'The Arrow' Yeats, W. B., {1903} *In the Seven Woods* (Macmillan), p. 20.

20   Sometimes, when I had gone to sleep... Yeats, W. B., {1972} *Memoirs* (Macmillan), p. 128.

21   Oh, Maud, why don't you marry me... MacBride, Maud Gonne, {1938, the conversation having taken place in 1913 }, *A Servant of the Queen: Reminiscences* (University of Chicago Press) pp. 318–319.

22   'No Second Troy', Yeats, W. B., {1912} *The Green Helmet and Other Poems* (Macmillan and Company), p. 12.

23   'Never Give All The Heart', Yeats, W. B., {1994} *The collected poems of W. B. Yeats* (Wordsworth editions), p. 63.

24   'He Wishes His Beloved Were Dead', Yeats, W. B., {1899} *The Wind Among the Reeds* (Elkin Matthews) p. 59.

25   At first every man on whom she looked...Tynan, Katharine {1913} *Twenty-Five Years: Reminiscences* (Smith, Elder & Co) p. 319.

26   What end will it all have? Yeats, W. B., cited in MacBride White, Anna and Jeffares, Norman A. (eds.) {1992} *Always Your Friend: The Gonne–Yeats Letters*, 1893–1938 (Hutchinson), p. 35.

27   As for Willie Yeats... Maud Gonne, cited in Balliet, Conrad {1979} *'The Lives and Lies of Maud Gonne' Eire—Ireland 14* (Fall 1979), 17–44, p. 32.

Bibliography

Works by W.B. Yeats:

Yeats, William Butler, *Memoirs: Autobiography--First Draft, Journal* {Macmillan, 1956}

Yeats, William Butler (Author), Richard Finneran (Editor)
The Collected Works of W.B. Yeats, Volume I: The Poems {Scribner, 2010}

Yeats, William Butler (Author), William O'Donnell (Editor),
Archibald, Douglas (Editor), *The Collected Works of W.B. Yeats, Volume III: Autobiographies* {Scribner, 2010}

other works:

Brady, Margery *The love story of W.B. Yeats and Maud Gonne*
{Mercier Press, 2004}

Brown, Terence *The Life of W.B. Yeats*
{Wiley-Blackwell, 2001}

Cardozo, Nancy *Lucky Eyes and a High Heart: The Life of Maud Gonne*
{Bobbs-Mervill, 1978}

Colum, Mary *Life and the Dream*
{Macmillan 1947}

Ellman, Richard *Yeats: The Man and the Masks*
{Faber, 1948}

Foster, Roy *The Apprentice Mage, 1865–1914 (W.B. Yeats: A Life, Vol. 1)*
{Oxford University Press, 1997}

Gonne MacBride, Maud *A Servant of the Queen*
{Colin Smythe Limited, 1938}

Greer, Mary K. *Women of the Golden Dawn: Rebels and Priestesses – Maud Gonne, Moina Bergson Mathers, Annie Horniman, Florence Farr*
{Inner Traditions Bear and Company, 1996}

Hardwick, Joan *The Yeats Sisters: a Biography of Susan and Elizabeth Yeats*
{Pandora,1938}

Hassett, Joseph M. *W.B. Yeats and the Muses*
{Oxford University Press, 2010}

Levenson, Samuel *Maud Gonne: A Biography of Yeats' Beloved*
{Littlehampton Book Services Ltd., 1977}

MacBride White, Anna ; Jeffares, A. Norman (Editors)
Always Your Friend: The Gonne–Yeats Letters 1893–1938, {Hutchinson, 1992}

Martyn, Edward 'A plea for the revival of the Irish Literary Theatre',
{*The Irish Review (Dublin)* Vol. 4, No. 38, Apr., 1914}

McCoole, Sinéad *No Ordinary Women: Irish Female Activists in the Revolutionary Years 1900–1923* {O'Brien Press; 2nd edition 2004}

Payne, Steven *Carrying the Torch* {Xlibris Corporation, 2010}

Quin, James; Ní Dhuibhne, Éilís; McDonnell, Ciara *W.B. Yeats Works & Days: A book to accompany the Yeats Exhibition at the National Library of Ireland* {National Library of Ireland, 2006}

Tynan, Katharine *Twenty-five Years: Reminiscences*
{London: Smith, Elder & Co, 1913}

Ward, Margaret *Maud Gonne*
{Thorsons; New edition, 1993}

Young, Ella *Flowering Dusk: Things Remembered Accurately and Inaccurately* {Longmans, Green and Co., 1945}

online sources:

National Library of Ireland, *Online Exhibition of the Life and Works of W.B. Yeats:*
{ http://www.nli.ie/yeats/ }

Sheila O'Malley, *"But one man loved the pilgrim soul in you."*
– Happy Birthday, Maud Gonne
{ http://www.sheilaomalley.com/?p=61120 }

The Free Library, *Yeats and Maud Gonne: (auto)biographical and artistic intersection.*
{ http://www.thefreelibrary.com/Yeats+and+Maud+Gonne%3A+(auto)biographical+and+artistic+intersection.-a0122700725 }

Acknowledgements

Eoin Purcell, *New Island Books*

Theo Dorgan

Carol Maddock, *National Library of Ireland*

Senator David Norris

His Excellency President Michael D. Higgins

John Ryan, *broadsheet.ie*

Cathal MacCoille, *RTE*

James C. Harrold, *Galway City Arts Officer*

Lorna Siggins, *The Irish Times*

Frank McNally, *The Irish Times*

Fidelma Mullane

Sheila O'Malley

Stella Mew, *The Yeats Society of Ireland*

Thomas C. Foley, *Former United States Ambassador to Ireland*

Melissa C. Danforth, *United States Embassy*

Honora Faul, *National Library of Ireland*

Rev Dr. Norman E. Gamble, Hon Archivist, *Irish Railway Record Society*

Stephen O'Brien, *The Sunday Times*

Paul Maher, *www.policehistory.com*

Declan Lowney

Seamus Cassidy

Barry Devlin

Brian Leyden

Mark Neiland

Jeananne Crowley

Damien Brennan, *The Yeats Society of Ireland*

Ian Kennedy, *The Yeats Society of Ireland*

Alan, Amy, Bob and Elizabeth West.